Allen Ginsberg

GAY SUNSHINE INTERVIEW

with Allen Young

Grey Fox Press

Bolinas, California

Grateful acknowledgment is made to Corinth Books for permission to reprint "In Society" from *Empty Mirror.*

ISBN: 0-912516-05-4

Allen Young is co-editor, with Karla Jay, of a gay liberation anthology, *Out of the Closets: Voices of Gay Liberation* (Douglas Books).

Distributed by Quick Fox, 33 West 60th Street, New York, N.Y.

Third printing, 1978.

INTRODUCTION

I first heard about Allen Ginsberg during my senior year at Fallsburgh Central High School in the Catskill Mountains borscht belt. One of my classmates brought a copy of *Howl* to our English class, and excerpts were read aloud. This same classmate – at last report he was a script writer for the Glen Campbell Show – also introduced me to Tom Lehrer and to the Weavers, bringing their albums into class for us to listen to. He was also the first boy I ever went to bed with; it was exciting and very sexy but we were both too repressed to become lovers. That was 1957, and I was 16 years old. As I recall it, the Weavers made more of an impact on me than Allen Ginsberg, perhaps because the Old Left household I grew up in was more tuned in to the simple message of folksy singers than to the images of hipster/faggot poetry.

One fall day in 1958, only a few weeks after I began my freshman year at Columbia, a friend told me that there was going to be an interesting poetry reading that night – Allen Ginsberg and Jack Kerouac were the featured poets. Get there early, he said. It was quite an event, though I didn't realize its importance until I saw McMillin Theatre (capacity 1200) quickly fill up while hundreds more milled outside and pounded on the doors. As the evening progressed, I came to understand that these two Columbia alumni, emerging culture heroes of a new generation, had been vilified and persecuted by the literary magnates who ran the Columbia College English Department. One member of that department, F.W. Dupee, defied his colleagues and appeared on stage as Master of Ceremonies to welcome Ginsberg and Kerouac back to Morningside Heights. I remember distinctly the sight of Professor Dupee, impeccably dressed in a dark suit, saying in his broad British accent, "The last time I was on this stage for a poetry reading, it was for T.S. Eliot." The audience snickered, presumably because there was something very un-T.S. Eliot about the unkempt trio sitting on chairs behind Dupee. As it turned out, Kerouac did not attend. Ginsberg brought along a friend, an unknown poet who he introduced merely as "Orlovsky," and the third person was Gregory Corso.

I think I was more turned on to Gregory Corso, perhaps because of an anti-war poem he recited, than to Ginsberg. In fact, I remember cynically questioning in my mind Ginsberg's tearful emotional outpouring as he recited "Kaddish." Other people who were at the reading were extremely moved by Ginsberg's rendering of "Kaddish," so I can only assume that my reaction (or lack of it) was a product of how turned off I was at the time to my feelings and the feelings of others. As I recall it, for many of us, the most interesting aspect of the poetry reading was the fact that the poets had not only forsaken jackets and ties, but were "slovenly" in appearance. My own gayness was strongly repressed at the time and I think I had no awareness that I had this special bond with the men on the stage. While the appearance of Ginsberg, Orlovsky and Corso may have had a transcendental impact on some of the people in the audience, I'm sure they were few in number. America, and the Columbia campus, was still feeling the deadening effects of McCarthyism. The peak of Columbia's cultural and political awakening was a full decade away, but, come to think of it, perhaps the appearance of this trio was its beginning. At the time, I was more interested in listening to folk music, reading the *National Guardian*, working my way up to becoming editor-in-chief of the *Columbia Daily Spectator*, and writing and handing out leaflets for the Student Committee for a Sane Nuclear Policy. The hipster poets just didn't seem to fit into my spheres of interest, perhaps because I was used to things being more structured.

In the fall of 1967, nearly a decade later, I met Ginsberg in person at the Liberation News Service (LNS) office/house on Church Street, only a few blocks from downtown Washington. We crossed paths again a couple of times during my involvement with LNS. He had already established some kind of friendly relationship with LNS founders Marshall Bloom and Ray Mungo, both of whom, unlike me, regarded Ginsberg as one of their culture heroes. (Ginsberg, as might be expected, has always been a supporter of the underground press.)

In the spring of 1968, Ginsberg returned to Washington to do a poetry reading in the gothic halls of Georgetown University, America's most prestigious Jesuit college. I joined other LNS staffers, as well as Georgetown members of Students for a Democratic Society (SDS) there, and we all felt the power of Ginsberg's poetical presentation (including the strongly anti-war "Wichita Vortex Sutra") before this audience of conservative-leaning collegians. I can remember in particular Ginsberg's deft responses during the question-and-answer period (we transcribed the tape and published it in LNS) – including Ginsberg's up-front and strong deflection of some silly fag-baiting jocks.

I was heavily involved with SDS during this period, and largely because of SDS's dogmatic approach to politics, and my own atheistic upbringing, I tended to dismiss Ginsberg's pacifism and his Buddhist/mysticist sensibility. In 1968 and 1969, while SDS reveled in the notion of the street-fighting man, Ginsberg was sitting cross-legged chanting "Om." Ginsberg – the pacifist, the Buddhist, the faggot, and most of all the human being – testified at the Conspiracy trial in Chicago. Prose cuting Attorney Tom Foran, already famous for his "freaking fag revolutionary" comment, tried to use Ginsberg's homosexual poems to discredit him, but Ginsberg's dignity and good humor won the day. When the poet got off the stand, Foran said, "that goddam fag . . ." Though I have always remained rather ambiguous about pacifism and rather aloof from spiritual matters, I think it was the beauty and honesty of this testimony that brought me close to Allen Ginsberg for the first time.

Another specific recollection I have about Allen Ginsberg from the 1960s is the *Playboy* interview he did in 1968 [issue of April 1969]. I was not a regular reader of *Playboy*, but I happened to see a copy, and while leafing through it I discovered the Ginsberg interview and in particular his affirmative comments about being gay. I can remember that it made me feel good; at the time, I was secretly involved in the gay scene but I wouldn't dream of telling my straight friends, much less of appearing in print, as did Ginsberg, as an openly gay person.

My experience with the Gay Liberation Front (GLF) in 1970 and 1971 helped me forge a new, strong, gay identity, and with that came an entirely new outlook not only on life itself, but also on politics and culture. By chance, while living on a gay communal farm in upstate New York in the summer of 1971, I picked up a copy of Jack Kerouac's *Dharma Bums* – an old paperback edition with its titillating cover referring to "yab-yum orgies" (a rather minor aspect of the novel). Around the same time, I discovered that Ginsberg was staying on a farm – purchased a few years before – located in Cherry Valley, N.Y., only 20 miles away. Both farms stood within a few miles of the shores of Lake Otsego, ceremonial birthplace of the Iroquois nation.

Upon reading *The Dharma Bums*, I was surprised to discover that the novel portrays Ginsberg (as Alvah Goldbook) as a heterosexual. I wondered why. I wrote Ginsberg a letter, inquiring about Kerouac's characterization of him in *The Dharma Bums*, suggesting the possibility of exchanging neighborly visits between our Otsego County farms, and asking him if he would be willing to be interviewed for a gay liberation newspaper. We didn't manage to get together that summer, but Ginsberg's response was very favorable, and, finally, in late September of

1972, a full year later, I arrived at the Cherry Valley farm. The goldenrod, a tiny yellow wildflower people seem to prefer to call a weed, was in full bloom.

Several of Allen's friends, who shared the house with him, greeted me when I arrived, and told me that Allen was waiting in the kitchen of the old farmhouse. Allen was very friendly, and immediately we began a conversation in which he expressed as much interest in me and my life as I did in his. For a few moments, he interrupted the conversation to show me around the house. As we passed an ancient pedal organ, he sat down and played chords while intoning a spontaneous poem about my visit and our shared gay consciousness. Sadly, my tape recorder was not yet going, so that particular bit of Ginsberg creativity has not been preserved. Then we spent more than an hour walking around the land, with Allen indicating the various features of the ecologically sound farm, including the absence of electricity and an ingenious water-pumping device known as a hydraulic ram. We picked some cherry tomatoes from the garden, shared reminiscences about the 1958 Columbia poetry reading I referred to earlier, and began to exchange viewpoints and experiences from our respective political and cultural backgrounds.

I soon became frustrated and nervous about not having the tape recorder with me, so we returned to the kitchen and began the interview. After transcribing the tapes in the following weeks, I submitted the 78-page transcript for editing to Winston Leyland, coordinator of *Gay Sunshine*, a San Francisco gay liberation periodical. Incorporating only a few minor corrections obtained over the telephone from Allen Ginsberg, *Gay Sunshine* published the interview in issue no. 16, January 1973. Prior to the publication of this Grey Fox Press edition, the interview (or excerpts from it) also has appeared in the *Berkeley Barb*, the *Real Paper* (Cambridge, Mass.), the *Georgia Straight* (Vancouver) and the *International Times* (London).

— Allen Young
Westwood, Mass.
April 11, 1973

GAY SUNSHINE INTERVIEW

YOUNG: One of the things that provoked this whole conversation between us was my reading of *The Dharma Bums* last summer. In that book the character Alvah, who is quite obviously you, is portrayed by Kerouac as heterosexual. There are a number of sexual encounters and there isn't any indication that there was any kind of homosexuality in this group of people.
GINSBERG: That was Kerouac's particular shyness. You know, I made it with Kerouac quite often. And Neal, his hero, and I were lovers, also, for many years, from 1946 on, on and off, at least I wanted to be, and we got to bed quite often, we didn't really fully . . . finally he didn't want any more sex with me, he rejected me! That's what he did! But we were still making it in the mid-1960s after having known each other in the mid-40s, so that's a pretty long, close friendship – Neal and Jack, for that matter.
YOUNG: Did Jack Kerouac identify himself as being a gay person?
GINSBERG: No, he didn't. A lot of that took place in the cottage we all held together, and then I had been living with Peter for several years. Peter, Jack, Gary [Snyder] and I and various other people were all sleeping with one or two girls that were around. Jack saw me screwing and was astounded at my virility. I guess he decided to write a novel in which I was a big, virile hero instead of a Jewish Communist fag.
YOUNG: What was your reaction to that? Did you feel that he was hiding?
GINSBERG: I didn't notice. *On the Road* has one scene in the original manuscript in a motel where Dean Moriarty screws a traveling salesman with whom they ride to Chicago in a big Cadillac; and there's a two line description of it which fills out Cassady's character and gives it dimension. That was eliminated from the book by Malcolm Cowley in the mid-50s, and Jack consented to that. So Jack actually did talk about it a little in his writing.

In a book that's being published now, *Visions of Cody*, there's a longer description of the same scene. It was written in 1950-51 by Kerouac and was his first book after *On the Road*, a sequel to it. It was a great experimental book, including a couple of hundred pages of taped, transcribed conversation between him and Neal, over grass at midnight in Los Gatos or San Jose, talking about life to each other, the first times they got laid, and jacking off, and running around Denver.
YOUNG: Why is it first coming out now?
GINSBERG: Kerouac always wanted it published. But the commercial

publishing world wasn't ready for a book of such great looseness and strange genius and odd construction. It's more like a Gertrude Stein *Making of Americans* than it is speedy Kerouac.

YOUNG: Was it a fight for Kerouac to get his stuff published?

GINSBERG: Oh, yeah. *On the Road* was written in 1950 and was never published till 57, even though he had previously published his great book, *Town and the City*. The commercial insistency was that he write something nice and simple so everybody could understand it, to explain what the beat generation was all about. So he wrote *The Dharma Bums*, to order, for his publisher, a sort of exercise in virtuosity and bodhisattva magnanimity. He wrote in short sentences that everybody could understand, describing the spiritual revolution as he saw it, using as a hero Gary Snyder; actually, "Japhy Ryder" is Gary Snyder.

YOUNG: So then your portrayal as a heterosexual doesn't have anything to do with being in the closet.

GINSBERG: No. I came out of the closet at Columbia in 1946. The first person I told about it was Kerouac, cause I was in love with him. He was staying in my room up in the bed, and I was sleeping on a pallet on the floor. I said, "Jack, you know, I love you, and I want to sleep with you, and I really like men." And he said, "Oooooh, no . . ." We'd known each other maybe a year, and I hadn't said anything.

At that time Kerouac was very handsome, very beautiful, and mellow – mellow in the sense of infinitely tolerant, like Shakespeare or Tolstoy or Dostoevsky, infinitely understanding. So in a sense – there's a term that I heard Robert Duncan use for poetry and I've heard others use for relation between guru and disciple – as a slightly older person and someone who I felt had more authority, his tolerance gave me *permission* to open up and talk, you know cause I felt there was space for me to talk, where he was. He wasn't going to hit me. He wasn't going to reject me, really, he was going to accept my soul with all its throbbings and sweetness and worries and dark woes and sorrows and heartaches and joys and glees and mad understanding of mortality, cause that was the same thing he had. And actually we wound up sleeping together maybe within a year, a couple of times. I blew him, I guess. He once blew me, years later. It was sort of sweet, peaceful.

YOUNG: Did you experience any kind of a split between your hipster circle and getting involved with other gay people as you were coming out?

GINSBERG: It's in a poem ["In Society"] that I read at the Chicago 7 trial. This is a dream I had in 1947 while I was at Columbia:

I walked into the cocktail party
room and found three or four queers
talking together in queertalk.
I tried to be friendly but heard
myself talking to one in hiptalk.
"I'm glad to see you," he said, and
looked away. "Hmn," I mused. The room
was small and had a double-decker
bed in it, and cooking apparatus:
icebox, cabinet, toasters, stove;
the hosts seemed to live with room
enough only for cooking and sleeping.
My remark on this score was under-
stood but not appreciated. I was
offered refreshments, which I accepted.
I ate a sandwich of pure meat; an
enormous sandwich of human flesh,
I noticed, while I was chewing on it,
it also included a dirty asshole.

More company came, including a
fluffy female who looked like
a princess. She glared at me and
said immediately: "I don't like you,"
turned her head away, and refused
to be introduced. I said, "What!"
in outrage. "Why you shit-faced fool!"
This got everybody's attention.
"Why you narcissistic bitch! How
can you decide when you don't even
know me," I continued in a violent
and messianic voice, inspired at
last, dominating the whole room.

There were a whole group of queens around Columbia at that time who were doing things like going down to hear Edith Piaf sing at the Plaza Hotel and interested in status and money. They had cultural interests that went back to Lotte Lenya and things like that, but at the same time it was an overly aristocratic, elitist thing.

YOUNG: Did you associate that with the faculty at Columbia also?

GINSBERG: There were a couple of guys on the faculty at Columbia that participated in that sense of things rather than in an open democratic Whitmanic gaiety, because to be open and democratic and Whitmanic meant, like, open, friendly, kissing the football players! In public, no less. Whereas the closet queen gaggle could get together and go down to the Plaza . . . .

YOUNG: Well, was kissing the football players in any sense a reality, or just a Whitmanesque fantasy?

GINSBERG: I was kissing Jack Kerouac, who was on the Columbia varsity team in those years. It was a Whitmanesque fantasy, which, like all Whitmanesque fantasies, were practical realities. Of course, then a faculty guy probably couldn't do it, but nowadays a faculty guy could.

I was silent about it [homosexuality] at Columbia the first year I was there, between the ages of 16 and 17. At 17 something shook me loose from the authoritarianism of the culture and from the authority of Columbia. I think it was the jailing of a friend, who I loved, who knew Jack well. And then also I was interested in Rimbaud and Whitman, and I had met Burroughs by then. I was getting teaching from Burroughs that included Blake and Spengler (*The Decline of the West*); and Semantics was important, separating words from the objects they represent, not getting confused by labels, like gay or queer, in those days.

So it was just a whole change, growing up out of high school and puberty and closed-in-ness. It wasn't closet; it didn't have that much style about it. It was just timidity and fear of rejection. All through high school I was secrtely in love with all sorts of boys – particularly one boy from East Side High, Paterson, who I actually followed to Columbia.

YOUNG: Whose name begins with "R." You mention him in one of your poems.

GINSBERG: Yeah. Very soon I was babbling at great length. The permission for that openness came from Burroughs and Kerouac, who I was living with. They were wide-brained, international, hip, Jack London, Doctor Mabuses, all.

Kerouac was a very funny, strange, heroic figure, a seminal figure for many ideas and attitudes. He had a lot of trouble; he drank himself to death. And he ended, like many older writers, reactionary in a funny, interesting, characteristic way, a way that's teaching rather than negative. But the basic thing about him as Character, with a capital C, was an enormous mellow, trustful tolerance and sensitivity. And that's why he's such a great writer and observer. You know, he held everything

dear, as a sensitive young fellow, even my fairy woes. In fact, we wound up in bed together.
YOUNG: You're saying that this really wasn't where he was at sexually?
GINSBERG: Well, he was very mixed sexually. He had a lot of trouble with attachment to his mother and his mother's dependence on him. He was a football player, and he liked girls. He liked to eat girls and was really hung up on them. That's what really excited him: black panties! black stockings! He also appreciated beautiful boys and had a really novelistic, personal appreciation of older queens – which was like a sharing of common humanity, and a sharing of emotions, even a sharing of the erotic, except that he didn't feel it was right for him to participate in the erotic.

As a novelist, he opened himself to the art of gaiety and some of its attitudes and styles in writing. In some of his poems there's a lot of stuff about himself, where there's all sorts of high teacup bullshit. In those days "high teacup" was a lifted pinky infra-language. I'm saying he had mixed feelings at different times, but I think it would have been abusive of his character to point an accusing finger and say, "You're a fairy!" There was a certain tendency among gay people there to plaster labels over everybody, including themselves, instead of seeing the nameless love that everybody is. Just as there was a tendency among macho heterosexuals to plaster labels, so there was a counter-balancing tendency among homosexuals to overreact to that and camp too heavily, so that he was sensitive about being put down as a fairy, which he wasn't. [*Calling over to Peter Orlovsky on the other side of the room where he was not listening to the interview:*] Was Jack a fairy?
ORLOVSKY: Huh?
GINSBERG: Was Jack a fairy?
ORLOVSKY: Was Jack a fairy? No . . . in a tiny sense of the word.
GINSBERG: Perfect, in a very tiny sense of the word. [*To Peter:*] We all made it with Jack once.
ORLOVSKY: [One time] he was so drunk he couldn't even get it up.
GINSBERG: [*Laughs*] Yeah. Well, no he came that time. We were at Clellon Holmes', remember? I blew him and you screwed me.
ORLOVSKY: What about on Second St.? Do you remember that? Jack was gallantly drunk, laying in one of the small, side rooms, and you tried to blow him. He couldn't get it up and he was talking about his little cock; it was so tiny, so small, shriveled up, sad.
GINSBERG: He was very apologetic. But ten years ago he was asking

me to blow him all the time. In 64-65 he said: "I'm old, ugly, red-faced, I'm beer-bellied and I'm a drunk and nobody loves me anymore. I can't get girls, come on and give me a blow job." There were times he'd get drunk and be really insistent on it. By that time he'd gotten beer-bellied, florid-faced, and I no longer saw him as the romantic, handsome, young glamor-beau of post-war, dark, doomed, maddened Spengler hippie-dom.

So, I got freaked out at the whole idea of bodies and sex, in fact. That was one of my first lessons in chastity. There's a line in Yeats: "Old lovers yet may have all the time denied, grave is heaped on grave that they be satisfied." I found actually in the course of time that everybody I really loved and wanted to go to bed with, I finally did. It may have taken twenty or thirty years, and we may have both fallen into ruins and baldness and all our teeth fallen out, but desire always found its way, even if it took decades. There's a lesson there. Once you become a little detached, once you lose neurotic, obsessive attachment, then, when things are floating lightly, then you find love objects that you once worshipped drifting in on the tide, back to you, more than you can deal with; in fact, horrifyingly rottened up from the sea.

An element in the gay lib struggle and metaphysics that I don't think has yet been taken up is that of disillusionment with the body. I'm not trying to be provocative in that – just the age-old realization of over-40, over-50, and over-60, and over-70 and over-80, finally, the age-old grinning skeleton, with the spiritual lesson behind it, of detachment from neurotic desire. I think there's a genuine eros between men that isn't dependent on neurotic detachment and obsession, that's free and light and holy and lambent – which is more or less what we all get during our first fantasies, loves and devotions. Some of us are lucky enough to be able to act out and receive back and forth. But it can only come in like the tide when you're free to float in it. If there's too much of a neurotic grasping to gaiety, to gayness, even to gay lib, than it makes eveything too tense, and the lightness of the love is lost. So the gay lib movement will have to come to terms sooner or later with the limitations of sex.

If you consider sex from a Hindu, Buddhist, Hare Krishna, even Christian fundamentalist viewpoint – a warning about the body and a warning about attachment itself – it becomes interesting. Burroughs has actually written about it at length in a way which hip people and even radicals have found very interesting: the sex "habit" – sex as another form of junk, a commodity, the consumption of which is encouraged by the state to keep people enslaved to their bodies. As long as they're enslaved to their bodies, they can be filled with fear and shock and pain and threat, so they can be kept in place. The road of that, he said, leads to the great palace of green goo, the garden of green goo, green goo trap, with everybody schlupping together in this green stuff.

I find, as I'm growing older, no less flutterings of delightful desire in my belly and abdomen. But also I'm becoming more tolerant of other resolutions between people besides sex. When I was in Australia, I had a crush on a beautiful young dobro player who traveled around with me. He sought me out and waited all day at my hotel and put himself at my service to play music with me. He wanted to play mantras and then turned out to be a great blues player, and he taught me blues. And he went to bed with me the first night, when I really got entranced by his . . . servility . . . and availability, and generosity, genius and sense of duty. And then he didn't want to go to bed with me after that, but he loved me. I was the first man he had ever been to bed with. How am I going to deal with somebody who really loves me but doesn't want to play with my cock and doesn't necessarily want me to blow him? But he didn't mind sleeping in bed naked with me, you know, because he loved me. There was a weird thing . . . but is that any more weird than my desires?

So I finally got into a scene which was like the old 19th century thing recommended by Edward Carpenter, and Whitman – people sleeping together. It's called "carezza," a platonic friendship in which people sleep together naked, caressing each other, but don't come, saving their seed for yogic or other reasons. So I did that with this kid.

For the next couple of weeks we were running around Australia. I found the intensity of my devotion to him in the heart area – a warm, aching feeling in the heart – growing and growing and growing, and becoming more and more desirous and narcotic-like, and more and more satisfactory to carry around with me. And I found him responding in a very similar way to me, and I realized that that same warmth was growing in his breast to me, and that what was building it was the naked chastity that we were practicing together. When we got on the stage and played together – I was singing mantras, blues and playing harmonium and he was playing dobro – the erotic communication between us got ecstatic and delirious. And it couldn't be withheld. We'd keep bursting out in song and eye glances which turned the audience on completely, and turned me on, and turned him on. So I was feeling another kind of very subtle, ethereal orgasm that seemed to occupy the upper portions of the body rather than the genital area.

Though I've always been prejudiced against that kind of sublimation, thinking of it as some sort of sublimation of primary, holy sex drives, the experience was so delicious that I can't really put it down for any moral reason at all. I recommend it; everyone should have that experience, too. You can get real close with people that you love who wouldn't otherwise want to sleep with you sexually. But you could have like a total relation. So there's all sorts, all forms . . . "Smash sexism!"

YOUNG: Actually I know some gay people who are thinking along those lines.

GINSBERG: Well, do you know heterosexual people who are thinking along those lines?

YOUNG: I know women who do.

GINSBERG: Well, I know lots of men . . . They may not want to sleep naked together but there's a love thrill in the breast thay have for each other, and yet are completely heterosexual. And I wouldn't be suprised if that *is*, among the mass of men, a universal experience, completely accepted, completely common, completely shared.

YOUNG: The whole idea of a buddy?

GINSBERG: The idea of a buddy is just the thin, label, vulgarization of it. The tradition of comradeship, of companionship, spoken of in the Bible . . . between David and Jonathan . . . all the way up to the body relationships as we know them . . . all these probably are intense love relationships which the gay lib group, in its political phase, has not yet accepted and integrated as delightful manifestation of human communication, satisfactory to everybody. In other words, there's a lot of political and communal development open to the gay lib movement as it includes more and more varieties of love, besides genital, and it may be that the bridge between gay liberation and men's liberation may be in the mutual recognition of the masculine tenderness that was denied both groups for so long.

YOUNG: In "Kaddish" you say something about the weight of your homosexuality: "Matterhorns of cock, Grand Canyons of asshole." Did you use those big metaphors because homosexuality was a heavy thing for you?

GINSBERG: When I was a sensitive, little kid, hiding, not able to touch anyone or speak my feelings out, little did I realize the enormous weight of love and numbers of lovers, the enormity of the scene I'd enter into, in which I finally wound up a public spokesman for homosexuality at one point. In that sense, "Matterhorns of cock, Grand Canyons of asshole." Taking off my clothes in public and getting myself listed in *Who's Who* as being married to Peter.

YOUNG: In a number of poems your homosexuality flows very naturally. Did that really happen?

GINSBERG: About 1953 I wrote a big, long, beautiful love poem to Neal Cassady called "The Green Automobile." I made the love overt. I didn't make the genital part overt but I made every other aspect: tenderness, kneeling together, holding on, travelling together, and then ultimate separation.

The next poem that had some overt thing was a little poem in 53-54, that mentioned the "culture of my generation, cocksucking and tears."

Living in Neal Cassady's house I wrote a little poem, from a line by Whitman, about lying down between the bride and the bridegroom. This was one of Whitman's great lines. In a fantasy I just wrote a description of what I would do, my love fantasy, between Neal and his wife, say, given permission by his tolerance.

The crucial moment of breakthrough in terms of statement came while writing "Howl": "let themselves be fucked in the ass by saintly motorcyclists, and screamed with joy." Usually the macho reaction to that image of being fucked in the ass would be just like in this new James Dickey film *Deliverance* where it's supposed to be the worst thing in the world.

YOUNG: You have a line somewhere: "who wants to get fucked up the ass, really?"

GINSBERG: That's in the book *Kaddish,* in a poem "Mescaline." On mescaline, who wants to exist in the universe to begin with? Who wants to have a name? Who wants to have an ego? And also who wants to be queer? Who wants the pain of being fucked in the ass at times when it is painful, when it occasionally is. That's part of the scene, too. Sometimes you never know it in advance. Things seem to be all right, and all of a sudden it turns out to be painful. So, who wants to be fucked in the ass that way, really?

The outrageous presentation came with "Howl," where I suddenly realized how funny it would be in the middle of a long poem, if I said: "Who let themselves be fucked in the ass . . . and screamed with joy," instead of "and screamed with pain." That's what the contradiction is in that line. An American audience would expect it to say "pain," but instead you have "and screamed with joy" – which is really true, absolutely, 100%.

And again I have a line like: "who blew and were blown by those human seraphim, the sailors, caresses of Atlantic and Caribbean love," referring to Hart Crane, actually. It was an acknowledgement of the basic reality of homosexual joy. That was a breakthrough in the sense of a public statement of feelings and emotions and attitudes that I would not have wanted my father or my family to see, and I even hesitated to make public. So that much was a breakthrough: literarily coming out of the closet.
YOUNG: Did critical reaction to you ever focus on the fact that you were homosexual?
GINSBERG: Yes, Norman Podhoretz, in *Partisan Review,* made a big attack on all the beatnik literature, the "know-nothing bohemians." He said that though my poetry was not too bad, its chief force rested on this somewhat questionable insistent proclamation of being queer, homosexual all the time, which, if frank, was not that interesting socially. It was a put-down which acknowledged and at the same time dismissed, while it called Kerouac a "brute."

Walt Whitman is very important on male tenderness. He's never been brought forth as a totem or as a prophet by either gay lib or by the radical left for some very precise statements he made on the subject of men's lib, this is in *Democratic Vistas,* or prospects for democracy, in which he's talking about how possibly materialistic competition in America will turn it into the fabled "damned of nations" – which it now has become. It may be that "we are on the road to a destiny, a status, equivalent, in its real world, to that of the fabled damned." It says, "Intense and loving comradeship, the personal and passionate attachment of man to man – which, hard to define, underlies the lessons and ideals of the profound saviours of every land and age, and which seems to promise when thoroughly develop'd, cultivated, and recognized in manners and literature, the most substantial hope and safety of the future of these states – will then be fully express'd."

Then in a footnote, he says:

> It is to the development, identification, and general prevalence of that fervid comradeship, (the adhesive love, at least rivaling the amative love hitherto possessing imaginative literature, if not going beyond it,) that I look for the counterbalance and offset of our materialistic and vulgar American democracy, and for the spiritualization thereof. Many will say it is a dream, and will not follow my inferences: but I confidently expect a time when there will be seen, running like a half-hid warp through

all the myriad audible and visible worldly interests of America, threads of manly friendship, fond and loving, pure and sweet, strong and life-long, carried to degrees hitherto unknown – not only giving tone to individual character, and making it unprecedently emotional, muscular, heroic, and refined, but having the deepest relations to general politics. I say democracy infers such loving comradeship, as its most inevitable twin or counterpart, without which it will be incomplete, in vain, and incapable of perpetuating itself.

Then, in the Preface to the 1876 edition of *Leaves of Grass,* he adds, in a long footnote:

> Something more may be added – for, while I am about it, I would make a full confession. I also sent out *Leaves of Grass* to arouse and set flowing in men's and women's hearts, young and old, (my present and future readers,) endless streams of living, pulsating love and friendship, directly from them to myself, now and ever. To this terrible irrepressible yearning, (surely more or less down underneath in most human souls,) – this never-satisfied appetite for sympathy, and this boundless offering of sympathy – this universal democratic comradeship – this old, eternal, yet ever-new interchange of adhesiveness, so fitly emblematic of America – I have given in that book, undisguisedly, declaredly, the openest expression . . . .
> Poetic literature has long been the formal and conventional tender of art and beauty merely, and of a narrow, constipated, special amativeness. I say, the subtlest, sweetest, surest tie between me and Him or Her, who, in the pages of *Calamus* and other pieces realizes me – though we never see each other, or though ages and ages hence – must, in this way, be personal affection. And those – be they few, or be they many – are at any rate *my readers,* in the sense that belongs not, and can never belong, to better, prouder poems.
>
> Besides, important as they are in my purpose as emotional expressions for humanity, the special meaning of the *Calamus* cluster of *Leaves of Grass,* (and more or less running through that book, and cropping out in *Drum-Taps,*) mainly resides in its Political significance. In my opinion it is by a fervent, accepted development of Comradeship, the beautiful and sane affection of man for man, latent in all the young fellows, North and South, East and West – it is by this, I say, and by what goes directly and indirectly along with it, that the United States of the future, (I cannot too often repeat,) are to be most effectually welded together, intercalated, anneal'd

into a Living Union.

So, that's really the direction, I think, for gay lib, for men's lib, the whole thing, you know, the release of emotions, finally a release of tenderness and that's the thing being suppressed.

YOUNG: Some people in the gay movement who call themselves "effeminists" would say that this sort of romanticization of masculine love is anti-woman, that it's another expression of male supremacy along the lines of Greek love; that the Greek society which tolerated and nurtured homosexuality was at its root a male supremacist society.

GINSBERG: I don't know. I don't think that's so in the long run. I think it's too genuine a feeling. With Whitman it didn't seem to interfere with his relations with women, because he had women friends who felt the same as he and who were, I think, married householder lesbians.

Whitman was saying that emotional giving between men, acceptance between men, has not been developed in America. One would say nowadays that it's been repressed by the spirit of competition and rivalry characteristic of capitalist home economics. A concomitant potential of a communal fraternality would be brotherly tenderness at least. That tenderness has been denied to the southern redneck and is responsible for his disrelation both with men and women. We don't yet know what the result would be of men forming closer emotional ties, or of the making conscious of those emotional ties and the acceptancy of them as a political significance.

What's the alternative? You can bring up the specter of Greek love and its anti-feminist concomitant and point out aspects of that in behavior of the beatniks – a fear of women, at least with me. But you would also have to see it as a real, heart-felt, native development, out of the fear and restrictiveness of the situation that we were brought up with: distrust, hatred, paranoia and competition between men rather than co-operation; and the same also between men and women.

Whitman was most sensitive and conscious of that because of his blocked love for men, because he couldn't make it with men openly and publicly. He had to find a way of expressing his adhesiveness, as he calls it.

I think a liberation of emotion between men would also lead to a liberation or straightening out of relations between men and women, because men would no longer have to be men in relation to women in the sense of hard and conquistador. They might have a much more relaxed relationship in which they weren't continuously obliged to be sexualized but could be just friends, or fond. Men's non-sexual friendship with women is now considered unmanly. So the development of frankly emotional, non-genital friendships with men might mean also the development, the opening up of frankly emotional non-genital friendships with women.

What is the effiminist alternative position between men? In other words, what do they propose besides saying, "No, you shouldn't feel good with your fellow man; heterosexuals should not develop toward emotional relations with heterosexuals?" They're pointing out the danger of an exclusive club, but we've already had that exclusive club in another form with the Hemingway macho scene, or with the military muscular macho scene. I'm saying and Whitman is saying that the antidote to the Hemingway macho and military macho scene is the development of frank, emotional tenderness and an acknowlegment of tenderness as the basis of genital or non-genital emotion. It may resolve itself in more men friendships, a democratization of friendships, so that it's not exclusively friendships between men and women on a sexual basis. I think it would resolve a lot of the macho conflict and contradictions.

I think that's one of the definitions of gaiety, or homosexuality: that there is a built-in conditioning, from every early times, in which both genital and emotional flow goes toward men more than, as is more usual, toward women. I thought the point of gay lib was to admit that variety of development as being viable, making a place for that. Otherwise, what is a homosexual? Unless you want to have a homosexual liberation front which proposes that men should develop out of homosexuality to a more equal and democratic relation with both men and women. But I think you could say: let the straight flower bespeak its purpose in straightness, which is to seek the light, and let the crooked flower bespeak its purpose in crookedness, which is to seek the light. The crooked flower has to go around the rock to seek the light. But the point was to get to the light of love, and the straight flower just grew up straight, right into the light of love. So you have either biological or conditional man-love and a gay lib movement which purports to release and make public those emotions. One thing that gay lib could do would be to break down the fear barrier that queens have against women. Breaking down the fear barrier between men and men would probably tend toward that.

Another point I'd like to take up is the traditional, effeminist possibly, objection to the "sexist" relations between older men and younger men. I saw some effeminist manifestos [on this point] in Berkeley. I took that question to Gavin Arthur, who died this year in San Francisco. He was a great gentleman, with beautiful manners, an astrologer, a teacher, a guru, and a grandson of President Chester Arthur. Neal Cassady slept with him occasionally, taking refuge in San Francisco from his travels with Kesey, back and forth from the railroad; and Gavin Arthur had slept with Edward Carpenter, and Edward Carpenter had slept with Walt Whitman. So this is in a sense in the line of transmission . . . that's an interesting sort of thing to have as part of the mythology. Kerouac's heterosexual hero who also slept with somebody who slept with somebody who slept with Whitman, and received the Whispered Transmission, capital W, capital T, of that love.

YOUNG: Kerouac's heterosexual hero? Who would that be?

GINSBERG: Neal Cassady, Dean Moriarty, who slept with Gavin Arthur, who slept with Edward Carpenter, who slept with Whitman. And I slept with Dean, so . . . So speaking from that line of transmission . . . what was whispered to me in that line of transmission by Gavin Arthur on the subject of older and young people making it: He says that's like an ancient thing, and it's very old and very charming for older and younger to make it – which you realize as you get old, too – and nothing to be ashamed of, defensive about, but something to be encouraged – a healthy relationship, not a sick neurotic dependency.

The main thing is communication. Older people have ken, experience, history, memory, information, data and also power, money and also worldly technology. Younger people have intelligence, enthusiasm, sexuality, energy, vitality, open mind, athletic activity – all the characteristics and sweet, dewy knowledges of youth; and both profit from the reciprocal exchange. It becomes more than a sexual relationship; it becomes an exchange of strengths, an exchange of gifts, an exchange of accomplishments, an exchange of nature-bounties. Older people gain vigor, refreshment, vitality, energy, hopefulness and cheerfulness from the attentions of the young; and the younger people gain gossip, experience, advice, aid, comfort, wisdom, knowledges and teachings from their relation with the old. So as in other relationships, the combination of old and young is functionally useful. It's far from sexist, in the sense that the interest of the younger person is not totally sexual; it's more in the relationship and the wisdom to be gained.

In Edward Carpenter's and Whitman's theory the older person made love to the younger person, blew the younger person, and there was the absorption of the younger person's electric, vital magnetism (according to a charming, theosophical, nineteenth-century theory). And it's something that somebody older like myself does experience as a natural fact. When you sleep with somebody younger you do gain a little vitality of breadth and bounce.

YOUNG: You've referred to Whitman and Edward Carpenter, and in some of your poems you mention García Lorca. For me it was a very recent discovery that these famous writers were gay like myself, that I had this bond with them. I'm curious as to how you made this discovery?

GINSBERG: Lorca's "Ode to Walt Whitman" speaks of "the sun singing on the navels of boys playing baseball under the bridges," which is an image of such erotic beauty that immediately you realize that he understood, that he was there; that was an emotion he felt. Then, later on I met somebody in Chile who knew him and said that he'd slept with boys. In fact, some sort of argument about a boy may be the cause of the shooting of Lorca. I don't think there's any written biographical history.

This sex epiphany is all in Whitman's texts, his homoerotic rhapsody, including a description of the time he lay down with a friend – it's in Part 5 of *Song of Myself*:

> I mind how once we lay such a transparent summer morning,
> How you settled your head athwart my hips and gently turn'd over
> upon me,
> And parted the shirt from my bosom-bone, and plunged your tongue
> to my bare-stript heart,
> And reach'd till you felt my beard, and reach'd till you held my feet.

YOUNG: You don't get it in high school.

GINSBERG: But school is irrelevant to poetry and everything else anyway. I mean school is something from the nineteenth century. Poetry has gone back to 15,000 B.C. There's Whitman's "We Two Boys Together Clinging":

> We two boys together clinging,
> One the other never leaving,
> Up and down the roads going, North and South excursions
> making,
> Power enjoying, elbows stretching, fingers clutching,
> Arm'd and fearless, eating, drinking, sleeping, loving,
> No law less than ourselves owning, sailing, soldiering, thieving,

threatening,
Misers, menials, priests alarming, air breathing, water drinking, on the turf or the sea-beach dancing,
Cities wrenching, ease scorning, statutes mocking, feebleness chasing,
Fulfilling our foray.

In "No Labor-Saving Machine" he writes:

But a few carols vibrating through the air I leave,
For comrades and lovers.

And Whitman says [in "A Glimpse"]:

A glimpse through the interstice caught,
Of a crowd of workmen and drivers in a bar-room around the stove late of a winter night, and I unremark'd seated in a corner,
Of a youth who loves me and whom I love, silently approaching and seating himself near, that he may hold me by the hand,
A long while amid the noises of coming and going, of drinking and oath and smutty jest,
There we two, content, happy in being together, speaking little, perhaps not a word.

Perfect! And real, absolutely real! That is actually life. That's even heterosexual life. That's the undescribable reality of human relationship in America. It can't be called gay . . . it's . . . that's something in the line of what I was talking about before in terms of what needs to be . . . the adhesiveness that Whitman spoke of that is latent in all of us now, and that's ready to be opened, and god knows how many, in the last ten years, how many younger boys that I've run across that I just sat and held hands with anyway and felt love feelings toward them and felt love feelings toward me, in situations like this which were maybe in a college, or somewhere, which had nothing to do with quote queer unquote, or even gay. Gay is too much of a category!
YOUNG: From what you said before, this existed to a certain extent with the bohemians or the hipsters . . .
GINSBERG: Oh, it existed back to Cro-Magnon man!
YOUNG: I think definitely a tension exists today between gay freaks and straight gays. There are some people in gay liberation who say, "I have

more in common with a heterosexual freak than with a gay person who's into very short hair and alcohol." And then there are other gay people who say, "My loyalty is to other gay people, and the freak culture is very macho."

GINSBERG: The form I felt it in was between the heartfelt, populist, humanist, quasi-heterosexual, Whitmanic, bohemian, free-love, homosexual tradition, as you find it in Sherwood Anderson, Whitman, or maybe Genet, a little, versus the privileged, exaggeratedly effeminate, gossipy, moneyed, money-style-clothing-conscious, near-hysterical queen. Of course, there's nothing more ancient or and in a sense honorable than the old shamanistic transvestite that we see running up and down Greenwich Avenue or, among the American Indians, a shaman who dresses himself up like a woman and even takes a husband. The screaming young queen – there's something very ancient and charming about that; great company, total individuality and expressiveness. Sometimes you fear it's the screaming, hysterical outside of somebody who's going to have a nervous breakdown and wind up in the church, or something. But then there's also the pettish, spiteful, anal retentive, disciplinarian.

But when I was younger the split was more between the grubby, beatnik, open-hearted . . . I couldn't call myself a fairy exactly . . . queer? . . . I have used that, but I've never found the right word . . . the nameless lovers, the nameless gnostic lovers . . . and the monopolistic queens, say, who had privilege and money. So that was the distinction. It was more between the cold-hearted and the warm-hearted.

YOUNG: In the gay bars of New York did you find both?

GINSBERG: Oh, I found both definitely. There were lots of outspoken, funny old sailor queens from the twenties; and then there were all sorts of prissy-mouthed, paranoiac, fearful, conservative-reactionary, short-hair, worried advertising martinets. And everything in between. There is a manneristic fairydom that depends on money, chic, privilege and exclusive, monopolistic high style, and I would say that it is usually accompanied by bitchiness and bad manners and faithless love, too. I like homosexuality where the lovers are friends all their lives, and there are many lovers and many friends.

YOUNG: Could you say something about your relationship with Peter Orlovsky?

GINSBERG: We met in San Francisco. He was living with a painter named Robert LaVigne in 54. I was having a very straight life, just trying it out, working in an advertising company, wearing suits, living up on Nob Hill in a nice big apartment with Sheila, who was a jazz singer and worked in advertising. Things were somewhat unsatisfactory between us. We'd been taking a little peyote, so we were into a psychedelic scene, too.

We got into an argument, so I wandered down one night into an area of San Francisco I'd never noticed then called Polk Gulch, now known as a notorious gay area with lots of gay bars. It was then more of a bohemian section, somewhat gay, artistic. Hotel Wentley was there, right on the corner of Sutter and Polk, and a Fosters cafeteria. I went and sat in the Fosters, late at night. I ran into Robert LaVigne and got into a big, interesting, artistic conversation about the New York painters I knew – Larry Rivers, de Kooning & Kline. LaVigne was a provincial San Francisco painter, so I was bringing all sorts of fresh poetry, art news from New York.

He took me up to see his place and his paintings, about four blocks away on Gough Street in an apartment that I subsequently lived in for many seasons and still use now. I walked into the apartment and there was this enormous, beautiful, lyrical, seven-by-seven foot square painting of a naked boy with his legs spread, and some onions at his feet, with a little Greek embroider on the couch. He had a nice, clean-looking pecker, yellow hair, a youthful teeny little face, and a beautiful frank expression looking right out of the canvas at me. And I felt a heart throb immediately. So I asked who that was, and Robert said, "Oh, that's Peter; he's here, he's home." And then Peter walked in the room with the same look on his face, a little shyer.

Within a week Robert said that he was going out of town or breaking up with Peter, or Peter was breaking up with him. He asked me if I was interested in Peter, and he'd see what he could arrange. I said, "Ooh, don't mock me." I'd already given up. I already had had a historic love affair with Neal Cassady a decade earlier. So I was already a tired old dog, in the sense of the defeats of love, not having made it, not having found a permanent life companion. And, in 1955, I was already 29. I wasn't a 20-year-old kid with romantic notions. That night we were in Vesuvios bar. Robert had a big conversation with Peter, asking Peter if he was interested, sort of like a *shachun*, a matrimonial arranger.

Then I went home one night. I went to Peter's room. We were to sleep together that night on a huge mattress he had on the floor. I took off my clothes and got into bed. I hadn't slept with too many people. Never openly, completely giving and taking. With Jack or Neal, with people who were primarily heterosexual and who didn't fully accept the sexualization of our tenderness, I felt I was forcing it on them; so I was always timid about them making love back to me, and they very rarely did very much. When they did, it was like blessings from heaven. If you get into it, there's a funny kind of pleasure/pain, absolute loss/hope. When you blow someone like that and they come, it's great! And if they touch you once, it's enough to melt the entire life structure, as well as the heart, the genitals and the earth. And it'll make you cry.

So . . . Peter turned around (he was in his big Japanese robe), opened up the bathrobe – he was naked – and put it around me and pulled me into him; and we got close, belly to belly, face to face. That was so frank, so free and so open that I think it was one of the first times that I felt open with a boy. Then, emboldened, I screwed Peter. He wept afterwards, and I got frightened, not knowing what I'd done to make him cry, but completely moved by the fact that he was so involved as to weep. At the same time the domineering, sadism part of me was flattered and erotically aroused.

The reason he wept was that he realized how much he was giving me and how much I was demanding, asking and taking. I think he wept looking at himself in that position not knowing how he'd gotten there; not feeling it was wrong, but wondering at the strangeness of it. The most raw meat of reasons, for weeping.

Then Robert hearing, seeing the situation, came in to comfort Peter a little bit. I was very possessive and I pushed Robert away. That got me and Robert into a funny kind of distrust that lasted for a year or two before our karmas finally resolved. He then realized he was well off on his own; and I was burdened with the karma of love.

Peter was primarily heterosexual, and always was. I guess that was another reason he was shocked – the heaviness of my sadistic possessiveness in screwing him. For the first time in my life I really had an opportunity to screw somebody else! I think that wounded him and thrilled me a little bit. So we still had to work out all that in our relationship over many, many years. It's painful sometimes.

We slept together perhaps one more time. Then I had to go to New York for my brother's wedding at Christmas, 54. I came back and moved into that apartment where they were living, at their invitation. And then there was a triangle of Robert, me and Peter. Peter had not made up his mind whether or not he wanted to make a more permanent relationship with me. I had my eyes on Peter for life-long love; [I was] completely enamored and intoxicated – just the right person for me, I thought. Robert was not sure he hadn't made a mistake, seeing the flow and the vitality that was rising up in both me and Peter. And Peter began withdrawing. He was caught in this rivalry between me and Robert, and, at the same time, there was his unsurety of me and his relation to me. Basically he liked girls anyway, so what was he doing lying there being screwed by me?

So I moved across from the Hotel Wentley and got a room. I was working in a market research job. I had the brilliant inspiration that all the categorizing and market research I was doing could be fed into a machine, and I wouldn't have to add all those columns any more. So I supervised the transfer for the company, and that left me out of a job just nicely, like a seamless occlusion. Then I got unemployment compensation.

I was being psychoanalyzed at Langley-Porter Clinic, an elite extension of U.C. Berkeley Medical School. He was a very good doctor, and I said: "You know, I'm very hesitant to get into a deep thing with Peter, because where can it ever lead. Maybe I'll grow old and then Peter probably won't love me – just a transient relationship. Besides, shouldn't I be heterosexual?" He said, "Why don't you do what you want. What would you like to do?" And I answered, "Well, I really would just love to get an apartment on Montgomery St., stop working and live with Peter and write poems!" He said, "Why don't you do that?" So I said, "What happens if I get old or something?" And he replied, "Oh, you're a nice person; there's always people who will like you." – which really amazed me. So, in a sense he gave me permission to be free, not to worry about consequences.

So then I waited for Peter, and Peter stayed up at the Gough Street apartment and went to school. I got this room and started writing a lot and waited and waited for Peter. Neal Cassady came by a couple of times. I made it with Neal. I can remember one of the last really wild times I made it with him, because I had a room of my own and there was privacy, finally. He was lying there naked, and I was sitting on his cock, jumping up and down trying to make him come.

And I just waited and waited [for Peter]. There was nothing I could run after or pursue, because I couldn't claim anything by force. Things got too difficult where Peter was living, so he got a room himself in the Wentley, across the street from where I was. And there was embarrassment, coldness – not knowing where each other was, what we would do. I was waiting for him to make some sort of decision. A couple of times we drank a little to see if we could get over the low. We didn't sleep together at all, though I was longing to.

Then one day he was lying in bed, and he started crying again. He said,

"Come on and take me." I was too overwhelmed and frightened to even get a hard-on. I didn't know what to do. We both had our clothes on. I was afraid he was interpreting it as me screwing him again, rather than really just having each other. But that soon got resolved, and we moved in together, into an apartment in North Beach. We found an apartment, and it had a room for him, a room for me, and a hall between us; and a kitchen together. So that gave us both a little privacy, and, at the same time, we could make it when we wanted.

He was very moody, very sweet, tender, gentle and open. But every month or two months he'd go into a very dark, Russian, Dostoevskian black mood and lock himself in his room and weep for days; and then he'd come out totally cheerful and friendly. I found after a while it was best not to interrupt him, not to hang round like a vulture; let him go through his own yoga.

The key thing was when we decided on the terms of our marriage – I think it was in Fosters cafeteria downtown about three in the morning. We were sitting and talking about each other, with each other, trying to figure out what we were going to do, who we were to each other, and what we wanted out of each other, how much I loved him, and how much did he love me. We arrived at what we both really desired.

I'd already had visionary experience: an illumined audition of Blake's voice and a sense of epiphany about the universe. He had had an experience, weeping and lonesome, walking up the hill to his college, and having a sense of an apparition of the trees bowing to him. So we both had some kind of psychedelic, transcendental, mystical image in our brains and hearts.

We made a vow to each other that he could own me, my mind and everything I knew, and my body, and I could own him and all he knew and all his body; and that we would give each other ourselves, so that we possessed each other as property, to do everything we wanted to, sexually or intellectually, and in a sense explore each other until we reached the mystical "X" together, emerging two merged souls. We had the understanding that when our (my particularly) erotic desire was ultimately satisfied by being satiated (rather than denied), there would be a lessening of desire, grasp, holding on, craving and attachment; and that ultimately we would both be delivered free in heaven together. And so the vow was that neither of us would go into heaven unless we could get the other one in – like a mutual Bodhisattva's vow.

That's actually the Bodhisattva's vow – "Sentient beings are numberless, I vow to enlighten them all. Passions are numberless, I vow to quench them all, cut them all down. The nature of the dharma, the doors of nature are endless, I vow to enter every single one of them. Buddha path very high and long and endless – vow to follow through all the way – Buddha path, infinite, limitless, vow to go all the way through." Sentient beings, numberless, unnumbered – countless, vow to count every one, enlighten every single one of them. Basically a vow to be reborn as everybody, one after another, every stone, every leaf blade, vow to be every individual part of the universe at one time or another, and accept the fate of that particle, so to speak.

Well, this is like a limited version of that, almost intuitive, the vow to stay with each other to whatever eternal consciousness: him with his trees bowing, me with Blake eternity vision. I was more intellectual, so I was offering my mind, my intellect; he was more athletic and physical and was offering his body. So we held hands, took a vow: I do, I do, you promise? yes, I do. At that instant we looked in each other's eyes and there was a kind of celestial cold fire that crept over us and blazed up and illuminated the entire cafeteria and made it an eternal place.

I found somebody who'd accept my devotion, and he found somebody who'd accept his devotion and who was devoted to him. It was really a fulfillment of fantasy, to a point where fantasy and reality finally merged. Desire illuminated the room, because it was a fulfillment of all my fantasies since I was nine, when I began to have erotic love fantasies. And that vow has stuck as the primary core of our relationship. That's the mutual consciousness; it's the celestial social contract, valid because it was an expression of the desire of that time, and it was workable. It's really the basic human relationship – you give yourself to each other, help each other and don't go to heaven without each other.

There's this mythology of Arjuna, from the *Baghavad Gita*, getting to the door of heaven. He's got this little dog following him, and they say, you can come in but you can't bring your dog. And he says, well, no, if I can't go in with my dog, I won't go. And then they say, oh, come on, you can go in, just leave him behind, it's only a dog. And he says, no, I love my dog, and I trust that love, and if I can't bring that trust in, then what kind of heaven is this? And the third time, he says, no, no, no, I'll stay out and put the dog in heaven but I won't go in without the dog. I vowed to tears with my dog, I can't leave my dog alone. And so, finally, after the third time, the dog turns out to be Krishna, the supreme lord of the universe and heaven itself. He was only trying to get heaven into heaven. And his instinct was right. And our instinct was right. It was enough to bring us through very difficult times — all through the change of status, beat generation and fame, the alteration of social identity that fame entails.

Our relationship has lasted from 1954 to 1972. The terms have changed tremendously. Peter's gone through a lot of changes, and we've separated for a year at a time. And always come back. We've gone through a lot of phases of sleeping with people together, doing orgies together, sleeping alone together. Now Peter sleeps with a girl. I very rarely sleep with him. But the origin of our relationship is a fond affection. I wouldn't want to go to heaven and leave Peter alone on earth; and he wouldn't leave me alone if I was sick in bed, dying, gray-haired, wormy, rheumatic. He'd have pity on me. We've maintained our relationship so long that at this point we could separate and it would be all right. I think the karma has resolved and worn out in a sense.

The original premise was to have each other and possess each other until the karma was worn out, until the desire, the neurotic attachment, was satisfied by satiation. And there's been satiation, disappointment and madness, because he went through a long period of speed freakery in the mid-sixties which really strained things. We had times of hostile screaming at each other such as happens in the worst of homo- and heterosexual marriages, where people have murder in their hearts toward each other. That burned out a lot of the false emotion of youth, and the unrealistic graspings, cravings, attachments and dependencies. So he's now independent, and I'm independent of him. And yet there's an independent curiosity between us.

YOUNG: There were some vague stories going around about your visit to Cuba in 1965 and departure. I'd like to know more about what you did in Cuba and what you said that eventually got you deported.

GINSBERG: Well, the worst thing I said was that I'd heard, by rumor, that Raul Castro was gay. And the second worst thing I said was that Che Guevara was cute. The most substantial thing was that I went around wondering why their marijuana policy, as of 1965, was so down and unscientific. I didn't accept the answer I got which was that the Batista soldiers used to get high and shoot at them, because I didn't think that was true. By hindsight, it doesn't seem really relevant to their needs, but at the same time, the denial of marijuana doesn't seem relevant to their needs, either.

There was persecution of homosexuals in the primarily gay-oriented theater group at the time. Instead of finding a place for that, they tried to break it up and sent everybody out to the sugar cane fields to work. This was an attempt to humiliate them, to use sugar cane for humiliation rather than community. And it wasn't in the newspapers. It was a secret campaign, with all the young Communist League party hack, flag-waving kids, like the Nixonettes, so to speak, accusing everybody they didn't like of being faggots.

It was considered bad form to wear beards and long hair, even though that was the characteristic style of Castro and the liberators up on the main drag, La Rampa. People were being stopped by the police and busted for having long hair, accused of being existentialists and degenerates. A bunch of young kids belonging to a poetry group I knew, El Puente (The Bridge), were being bugged by the police, not allowed to publish, and were called fairies. One evening the whole group of Escritores del Encuentro Inter-Americana, sponsored by Casa de las Americas, went to the theater to hear a concert of "feeling" music. We were joined there by a whole bunch of young poet kids. When we left the theater, they were all stopped by the police, arrested and told to stop hanging around with foreigners. Some of the young poet kids were translating my work.

So there was this police bureaucracy in Cuba that was very heavy and was coming down heavy on culture, in terms of beards, sexual revolution tendencies, sociability, and homosexuality. In other words, there was no real cultural revolution; it was still basically a Catholic mentality. As in many Communist countries, the police bureaucrat Party hacks were like Mayor Daley ward-heelers: flag-waving, fat-assed square types. Self-seeking squares, not at all spiritually communist, were getting control of the police and emigration bureaucracies and setting themselves at odds against the people who screw with their eyes open, listen to the Beatles and read interesting books like Genet, and *fought* at the Bay of Pigs against the Americans. Even people who had been up in the mountains with Castro were very secretive about smoking grass. The press was monolithically controlled and boring, and the newspaper reporters for the press reminded me very much of the self-righteous newspaper reporters from the *Daily News* as far as their opinionation and argumentativeness.

I just continued talking there as I would talk here in terms of being anti-authoritarian. But my basic feeling there was sympathetic to the revolution. I had friends living there, was invited there as a guest, and I took part as a judge in a literary contest, and I just shot my mouth off! The worst thing was the talk about homosexuality and the challenge to the official position about it. Castro had taken an official position in a speech at the university in which he had attacked homosexuality. He called it degenerate or abnormal, saw it as a cabal, perhaps, a conspiracy. I think he praised the Young Communist League for turning in fairies.

I suggested to Haydee Santamaria that they invite the Beatles and got the answer: "They have no ideology; we are trying to build a revolution with an ideology." Well, that's true, but what was the ideology they were proposing? A police bureaucracy that persecutes fairies? I mean, they're wasting enormous energy on that. Some of those "fairies" were the best revolutionaries – people that fought at the Bay of Pigs, Playa Giron.

I slept with one young poet, secretively. I took one stick of grass one day, walking along a shady street with a bearded fellow who said he'd been up in the mountains with Castro and that they had smoked up there. But that was the extent of my "criminal behavior."

I thought one of the most brilliant and interesting results of gay liberation was the confrontation with the repressive, conservative police bureaucracy in Cuba. I think the confrontation between the Venceremos Brigade and gay lib showing the Cuban mental block on the subject of homosexuality was one of the most useful things that gay lib did on an international scale. At least it brought the question to front-brain consciousness. Gay lib people went there to offer themselves and, I think, less to confront the Cubans than to find out what the scene was. They were, obviously, faithful in terms of change and sympathy with the revolution. Since it was a gay lib group, the right wing, capitalist press couldn't take advantage of the confrontation to put shame on Cuba, because otherwise they'd have to defend gay lib! So, it was gay lib taking the bull by the horns, within the context of brotherhood, challenging the Cuban macho, repressive mentality in a constructive way. I don't think the Communist Party there reacted very well. What was the result?

YOUNG: In the interim period the brigade has adopted a policy of excluding gay liberation people. There was a fifth brigade that did not have gay liberation people on it. The Cubans have since come up with a detailed, rather specific policy statement on homosexuality, declaring it to be a "social pathology." The pro-Cuban Venceremos Brigade people have related with hostility to the radical gay lib movement. Large numbers of New Left people who formerly were very sympathetic to Cuba have reduced their expression of sympathy for Cuba because of the gay question. The Cubans, basically, have forced a lot of people to choose between the Cuban revolution and gay liberation, and they're quite surprised to find people choosing the gays.

GINSBERG: When Castro originally had his revolution, he said it's a marxist revolution but it's still a humanist revolution. If it's a humanist revolution, they cannot put down gays. Otherwise, it's double-talk. I think it's important to support any separation out from American imperialism and conspicuous consumption, and any sort of independence from American psychological domination. But, on the other hand, the reason for doing so is to become human again and independent.

If the definition of human and independent means sustaining an old, authoritarian viewpoint toward sexuality – the monotheistic, Catholic viewpoint – then it would be better that American radicals at least realized that they're dealing with human beings in the Cuban situation rather than with divine authorities. I am willing to accept the fact that the Cuban revolution is a genuine relief from Mafia capitalist domination, the previously corrupt society of Cuba, and a release from America.

In other words, I feel the Cuban revolution is important and should be supported. They'll learn, soon enough. They're gonna see the end of the world anyway and end up with long hair and pansexualities. They're going to have to take it as state policy before they're over, just to relieve their population problem. I think the gays are dealing in the long run from a position of great strength, because their position is founded in ancient rules of mammal behavior and ecological necessity as far as the future and the recognition of common humanity. So I think gays can afford to say, "Ahhh."

I saw a lot of other things there in terms of cultural persecution. I was interested in *santeria* [Afro-Cuban cults]. With a group of writers I went to a *santero's* house in the outskirts of Havana for a Congo ceremony and also for a Yoruba ceremony. In the middle of the ceremony the police came in, wanted everybody's name and address and harassed everybody. They said you had to have a permit for any meeting of more than ten or twelve people after a certain hour or even at any time in a private house. They knew who we were perfectly well; we had representatives there from the Casa de las Americas. So again it was the police bureaucracy hassling the cultural side.

One of the boasts in Cuba was the acceptance of black consciousness. The *santeria* religion was one of the great ancient tribal things that had resisted the white, honky, Christian church, and here they were interrupting this ceremony! There was apparently an attempt to discourage the practice of *santeria* because it was like a rival spiritual authority to the state.

In Cuba I remember that most of the honkies from a Catholic background were indifferent to black culture and to the heart of it which was the *santeria* cult. But among the appreciators were some of the old gay painters and poets.

YOUNG: A couple of friends of mine who were recently in Cuba told me that the persecution of the *santerias* continues. At the same time there is peace between the Cuban government and the Catholic Church. The Cuban Declaration of the Congress on Education and Culture specifically attacks the *santeria* but speaks very positively about relations with the Catholic Church, especially in terms of the support of the Catholic Church in other Latin American countries for left-wing forces.

One of these black *santeros*, who was wanted by the police, escaped and hid in the house of a homosexual friend. They were both caught and arrested. The news report about the arrest emphasized the connection between *santeria* and homosexuality. They used the stronger taboo against homosexuality to reinforce the attack on the *santeria.*

Edward Carpenter says that one of the things that made him a revolutionary was going to Africa and through his gayness becoming familiar with the humanity of the African people.

In Cuba I met the three people who run the puppet theatre, the Teatro de Guinol, a brother and sister and another fellow. The brother and the other fellow are both gay. The people in the theater are mostly gay. When I was there in 1969, I hardly even perceived that they were gay, because of my own closet situation. They told me they were producing a Yoruba play. Pepe Carril wrote it and it has been translated into English by Susan Sherman. Carucha, one of the directors of the theatre, told me that they had to fight to do this Yoruba play. They did a theatrical puppetry presentation of the Yoruba cult, and afterwards the party hacks thought that it was o.k.

GINSBERG: The original humanist, Marxist approach was that western monopoly capitalism, homogenized, turned into a commercial mass cult, a plastic, degenerate commodity. From a revolutionary point of view, the rights and cultural heritage of workers and minorities had to be preserved from the depredations of the evil banks and cultural monopolists. By revolutionary theory the Yoruba tradition among the blacks should be cultivated and subsidized, kept as folk art of the people, as their art and religion. So, it's a contradiction in basic marxist approach to have a rivalry between police bureaucracy and Yoruba priests.

YOUNG: I think it has something to do with plain old racism; white supremacy.
GINSBERG: I suppose so. It means that blacks have a culture of their own, and whites don't want that. So what do you say to Castro? Has anyone had an intelligent conversation with Castro in the last seven years? He used to have conversations with interesting people like Sartre.

I was in my hotel room one morning toward the end of my stay in Cuba when three uniformed, olive-clothed, mute soldiers came in with an officer. He said he was head of immigration, that I had to pack my bags, and that I was being deported on the next plane out, to Prague. I asked if they had informed the Casa de las Americas, and the answer was, no; there will be time enough later. They wouldn't let me make a phone call to the Casa, which was my host, and they took me downstairs. I shouted in the lobby to Nicanor Parra that I was being deported and they should get in touch with the Casa de las Americas and warn them. I was driven out to the airport. On the way I asked why I was being deported. The officer said, "For breaking the laws of Cuba." And I said, "What laws?" He responded, "You'll have to ask yourself that." And that answer, I thought, was like the answer I got from Dean McKnight at Columbia University when I got kicked out for staying overnight in my room with Jack Kerouac. And we hadn't made love at all. We just slept there because Kerouac had no place to sleep that night.

I didn't go round screaming to *Time* magazine that I'd been unjustly kicked out of Cuba. I just gave them the benefit of the doubt, understanding that I was like a pawn. It was a fight between the liberal groups and the military bureaucracy groups. I realized also that the more the United States put pressure on Cuba, the more power the right wing military, police bureaucracy and Party hacks would get. The real problem was to relieve the pressure in America, to end the blockade rather than to "blame" the Cuban Revolution, Castro, or Marxism – although I don't think Castro was very tactful on the question of homosexuality. There was an excessively macho thoughtlessness on his part, and insensitivity.
YOUNG: When I was there in 71 at the journalists' conference, there was a reception, at the side of a big swimming pool. Everybody was crowding around Fidel. He was loving it and getting involved in lively conversation with different people. I was feeling very out of it. I was the only male that didn't have short hair, a suit and a tie, except for some Africans in African dress. The whole idea of pushing into a crowd to talk to a famous

man was something I wasn't exactly into.

I decided to get involved in conversation with some other people. I spoke with a very important comandante, a black guy, who had fought with Fidel in the hills and was on the central committee. Karen Wald, an American who was with us, asked him what he thought about machismo. And he said, "Oh, man, that's good!" I can't figure out to this day whether he was putting her on or whether he was simply expressing his very gut reaction – which is that machismo is an important thing for a Cuban man to appreciate.

GINSBERG: The question does finally boil down to machismo, both here in the United States, and there, in terms of revolutionary tactics. Gay lib, in a sense, has a good approach to straight people with smug, middle-class ideas about power coming out of the barrel of anything, actually.

YOUNG: I think there's been a certain schizophrenia in the radical section of gay liberation. People have said they're against power. In fact, most of the people I know in the radical wing of gay liberation don't even like and don't use the slogan "gay power" because of the word *power.*

GINSBERG: Gregory Corso has a great poem called "Power" which I invite you to check out. It was written in 1959: "Standing on a street corner waiting for no one is Power" . . . "A thirst for Power is drinking sand."

YOUNG: On the one hand people were attacking the whole notion of power, trying to do away with power in personal relationships. On the other hand, there was this desire to be a part of the left, a desire best epitomized by the slogan, "Go left, go gay, go pick up the gun" – a variation of the Panther slogan.

GINSBERG: Though it may serve as a vehicle for machismo among gays, it also serves as a deflating slogan for the pompousness of black or white power slogans that are actually a bit ridiculous sometimes.

The slogan "Power comes out of the barrel of a gun" was irrelevant in the American situation all along. There wasn't enough imagination in terms of tactics and poetry. How do you transform and convert America? It was a sign of the poverty of imagination that finally people fell into violence, when all along the whole problem had been mental violence, blindness and rage. Gay lib really did turn all of the machismo of the left inside out.

YOUNG: Do you feel that gay liberation has influenced you personally

in any way?
GINSBERG: I use the word "gay" now which I never did before. And that's important when you change somebody's language. I find myself drifting toward the gay lib group whenever there's a big parade, because it's generally so sincere and interesting. The ideology there at least is personal. Gay lib has influenced my thinking on a few other things – like junkie liberation.

If you can have gay liberation from the oppression of the macho oppressors, then you can have junkie liberation from the oppression of the macho Mafia C.I.A. fuzz A.M.A., the Truman-Nixon oppression of punitive treatment of junkie illness rather than medical treatment. There should be a Junkie Liberation Front. They're the most oppressed group in America, in the sense that they're hunted down like dogs by people with guns. They're always under the threat of jail. They're sick. They've got a legitimate illness, and they're not being treated with legitimate medical means. But they are thrown over into the hands of the most corrupt police agents in America – narcs who have relations with the Mafia and peddle – as proved by the Knapp Commission and various other documented analyses. They've suffered the greatest image distortion of any group in America. There was never a category of human being in America that was invented as low as the fiend category for heroin addicts. They didn't even say liquor fiends.

And they are the victim of slander. They're called a criminal class, violent murderers when they're not; when it's the alcoholics who are really out of control.

YOUNG: Half of the Pentagon generals are alcoholics, too.

GINSBERG: So, I mean, there should be Junkie Liberation. The idea of the gay liberation front turned me on to the terminology Junkie Liberation Front. It added a little fillip to the relationship that Peter and I have.

YOUNG: One of the quotations that floats around gay liberation ascribed to you is your reaction to the Stonewall riot: "The fags have lost that wounded look." What were the circumstances?

GINSBERG: It was an interview in the *Village Voice.* I wasn't there at the riot. I heard about it, and I went down the next night to the Stonewall to show the colors. A crowd was there, and the place was open. So I said [to myself], the best thing I can do is to go in; the worst that can happen is I'll calm the scene. They're not going to attack them when I'm there. I'll just start a big Om.

I didn't relate to the violent part [of Stonewall]. The trashing part I thought was bitchy, unnecessary, hysterical. But, on the other hand, there was this image that everybody wanted to make that they could beat up the police, which apparently they managed to do. It was so funny as an image that it was hard to disapprove of, even though it involved a little violence.

YOUNG: Did you at that moment anticipate that this might lead to something called gay liberation with organizations, publications and so forth?

GINSBERG: It seemed to have been there all along, somehow. There was already that in rudimentary form with the Mattachine Society and One. They were more sedate, but they did some interesting things in their time.

I published the poem to Neal "The Green Automobile," in 1959 in *The Mattachine Review.* Because it was a frank love poem, approving of the [gay] love relationship, it brought forth a rebuke from psychiatrist Karl Menninger of Topeka, Kansas. He wrote a strange letter to the Mattachine Society, denouncing the poem and saying they were trying to cure everybody, and here was this terrible poem boasting of these perverted feelings!

I went to a few of Mattachine's meetings and gave a little peotry reading there in San Francisco. But I never got involved politically with them, just literarily. Of course, San Francisco was always more advanced then New York in terms of the acceptance of homosexuality. It's like a Parisian city. There was a historic, famous bar in San Francisco's North Beach, near what was called the Monkey Block [the Black Cat], which was maybe the greatest gay bar in America. It was really totally open, bohemian, San Francisco, Viennese; and everybody went there, heterosexual and homosexual. It was lit up, there was a honky-tonk piano; it was enormous. All the gay screaming queens would come, the heterosexual gray flannel suit types, longshoremen. All the poets went there.

YOUNG: Martha Shelley has a great first line in "Gay is Good," one of the first gay liberation articles: "Look out straights, here comes the Gay Liberation Front, springing up like warts all over the bland face of Amerika, causing shudders of indigestion in the delicately balanced bowels of the Movement." At the end of the article she says, "You will never be rid of us because we reproduce ourselves out of your bodies."

GINSBERG: There's too much of a conflict there. The point is that nobody's straight. It's like calling someone a pig. Everybody has dreams that have some homoerotic content. So the problem is to make it safe for "straights" to feel the whole spectrum of feelings instead of single level feelings, just as it's important for gay people to feel a whole spectrum of feelings. The politics of challenge in that sense doesn't seem to make too much sense. You don't woo somebody by challenging them. You woo them by giving them a place where they're comfortable, making it safe for them to get a hard-on . . .

YOUNG: I think there are definitely tensions in the movement now between the people who say having lots of blow jobs is liberation, and those who say that we are trapped in a meat-meets-meat approach and have to get out of that and relate to each other as people.

GINSBERG: It's an important human experience to relate to yourself and others as a hunk of meat sometimes. That's one way of losing ego, one holy divine yoga of losing ego: getting involved in an orgy and being reduced to an anonymous piece of meat, coming, and recognizing your own orgiastic anonymity. It's not a place where you want to live all your life, but it's certainly a place where you want to see and experience as a lesson, experience of consciousness that's valid for a certain level, an experience of great, divine beast consciousness. That's what they used to have the Dionysian orgy for; it's an ancient ritual; I don't think there's anything wrong with relating to people on the level of pure meat, as long as you don't get trapped into that all the time as a single level of consciousness – as some queens do.

The gay lib answer is obviously not going to be just simply lyrical sexuality. The use of sex as a banner to *épater le bourgeois*, to shock, show resentment or to challenge is not sufficiently interesting to maintain for more than ten minutes; it's not enough to sustain a program that will carry love through the deathbed or help out Indo-China. Or even get laid, finally. You have to have something more. You have to relate to people and their problems, too.

I dig baths and orgies. I think orgies should be institutionalized: impersonal meat orgies, with no question of personality or character or relating to people as people.

Anyone who insults Dionysus had better watch out! The leopards come and get them, or else they get turned to vine leaves, in Ezra Pound [Canto 2], when they practice god-slight, the insult to Dionysus.

YOUNG: The problem with that approach is that as long as your meat is young and attractive, you're doing o.k. But if it doesn't meet the standard . . . .

GINSBERG: When you get to be my age, that's when you really appreciate orgies, in the dark when nobody sees anybody and doesn't give a shit who they're being screwed by. The paranoia in Turkish baths, are you acceptable or not, is another problem. But orgy is one way for people to equalize – for fat people, thin people, handsome people and ugly people, hunchbacks and one-legged people and rachitics all together in the dark.

Peter and I used to get into scenes in San Francisco with girls and boys together, very nice. He liked girls, and that situation would set up a nice vibration when other men would come in. Since Peter and I were already close and making it, that opened the door to anybody. He'd make out with girls and I'd make out with boys. Sometimes I'd make out with girls too. Or we'd make out with each other. We had a two year period in San Francisco where almost every party we went to we took off our clothes and wound up in bed with one or two people. We didn't try to start orgies; we just took off our clothes, wandered around the party, had a good time and didn't make a big scene out of it.

YOUNG: When I saw the dedication of *Howl* and found out about Carl Solomon, I was curious as to your relationship.

GINSBERG: That was never an erotic relationship. I went to a mental hospital in 1948 as the result of a bust involving grass and stolen cars – a typical, college fuck-up bust. In the old days when you were from a genteel family they sent you off to a bughouse to get out of going to jail. So I went through that middle-class resolution to my bust. I wound up in the New York State Psychiatric Institute on 168th Street.

The day I walked in with all my bags I met this big fellow [Carl Solomon] just coming up from electric shock. I was waiting to be assigned a room, nervous and strange and wondering what I was doing in this psychiatric institute with all these people supposed to be crazy. And a little worried that I'd lost my grip on reality.

Carl Solomon asked me who I was. He seemed so intelligent and literate that I wanted to see if he had any soul. So I said, "I'm Prince Mishkin" (a saintly character in *The Idiot*.) And he said, "I'm Kiriloff (a hard nihilist in *The Possessed*). So we had a funny understanding. Then we had a literary time, writing imaginary letters to T.S. Eliot. He introduced me to Genet's work and to Artaud's work. He was very learned in French literature and surrealism. He turned me on to a lot of French literature that I'd missed. Then he took me down to the Village, and I began digging the whole subterranean Village of 1949-50 through his eyes. He's written several little collections of pithy *contes* – stories and aphorisms.

He's still a friend and was here about a month ago. A couple of times a year we get together and spend some time. He was heavily ideologically Marxist at one time and then anti-Marxist. He went through all sorts of chameleon-like mad changes, searching for a sane way of approaching the fact that everybody in the world is mad, anyway.

YOUNG: I remember hearing that around the time of the original excitement about LSD, Timothy Leary made some statement saying that it cured homosexuality. I recall you said you had a heterosexual experience under the influence of LSD.

GINSBERG: [I had] an emotionally heterosexual fantasy experience in relation to my mother and girls. But everybody has that on LSD. It was a breakthrough of heterosexual feeling/emotion in relation to my mother, and there were so many girls that I'd rejected. When Leary was looking around for information and rationalization on LSD, I told him that it probably would loosen up some of the blocks in homosexuality. The reverse is true, too: it would probably loosen up some of the blocks in heterosexuality, which it's notorious for doing. Leary or someone else carried the ball a little too far on that one, to say that I experienced heterosexual breakthrough for the first time in my life. I've got a venerable heterosexual or bisexual history to begin with.

In the context of the arguments about LSD I gave Congressional testimony:

> "One effect I experienced in Peru I would like to explain. From childhood on I had been mainly shut off from relationships with women, possibly due to the fact that my own mother was, from my early childhood on, in a state of great suffering, frightening to me, and [she] finally died in a mental hospital. In a trance state I experienced in a *curandero's* hut [in Peru] a very poignant memory of my mother's self, and how much I had lost in my distance from her and my distance from other later friendly girls. For I had denied most of my feelings for them out of old fear. And this tearful knowledge that had come up while my mind was opened through the native vine (some yage) did make some change toward greater trust and closeness with all women thereafter. The human universe became more complete for me, and my own feelings more complete . . . ."
>
> [*Hearings of the Special Subcommittee on the Judiciary, U.S. Senate, Senate Resolution 199, "LSD and Marijuana Use on College Campuses," June 14, 1966.*]

YOUNG: In your development as a yoga person, have you come across the somewhat anti-homosexual writings of certain yoga masters?
GINSBERG: No, I've never seen any of those. A couple of months ago I got into a conversation with a teacher I'm working with now, Chögyam Trungpa Tulku, incarnate lama, and asked him what he thought about homosexuality. He said he thought it was interesting. I asked him if he thought it was negative or bad. He said, "No, it doesn't make any difference what forms the bodies are; the important thing is the communication." This is very sensible, clear and really important. With communication overt, homosexual lovemaking is obviously terrific and charming. Without communication it's a drag, and heterosexuals the same.
YOUNG: I've always felt there was something particularly mystical about two men doing sixty-nine, something in the configuration of the bodies.
GINSBERG: Yes. There's a mysticism when you screw somebody in the ass, or in being screwed. There's a great mysticism in being screwed and accepting the new lord divine coming into your bowels – "Please Master." There's a great mysticism in a girl being screwed, or climbing on a guy. Any position is mystical.

The official answer of my Tibetan teacher was interesting: the quality of the emotion is important; communication is important. And the form is not, obviously.

There's a tradition against marriage in the Gelugpa, a yellow-hat sect of Tibetan Buddhism. It slowly evolved historically that the monks all make it with each other. But basically the bias, if any, in yoga is toward chastity, retention of sperm. Sperm is art, poetry, music, yoga. Sperm is *Kundalini*, serpent power: a shivering tingling that runs and takes over the top of your head and spreads throughout the whole body. Retention of sperm is apparently one of the basic understandings of some forms of yoga.

So it's not really homosexuality or heterosexuality that would be disapproved. It would be attachment to any kind of "pleasure," as a neurotic attachment. As Burroughs might say, an attachment to the green goo factory, an attachment to body. The body itself may be the by-product of a large scale conspiracy by certain forces as Burroughs says, trying to keep people prisoners in a prison universe made out of parent matter, subjected to appearances and apparent physical conditions defining their limitations. As Blake, the Buddhists, and Burroughs would say, the real world is a world of complete, blissful, empty silence. In other words, the anti-body yoga position is not anti-homosexual; it's pro-empty or pro-transcendental.

We are so free of our bodies that we are able to stay in them; and it's all right to be in them and use them. That's the Buddhist position. You're so free of the body you don't have to be afraid of it.

We have the question of what is sex, which William Burroughs has addressed himself to. He's one of the few gay lib "heroes," one of the few homosexual theorists who has theorized up to the point of outside-of-the-body, and detachment from sexuality. In fact, the cut-ups were originally designed to rehearse and repeat his obsession with sexual images over and over again, like a movie repeating over and over and over again, and then re-combined and cut up and mixed in; so that finally the obsessive attachment, compulsion and preoccupation empty out and drain from the image. In other words, rehearsing and repeating it over and over, and looking at it over and over, often enough. Finally, the hypnotic attachment, the image, becomes demystified. His particular sexual thing is being screwed, because Burroughs can come when he is screwed; he's one of the few men that can.

YOUNG: You mean without manipulating himself?

GINSBERG: Yeah . . . look, no hands!

YOUNG: I remember he has that image in *The Naked Lunch,* but I couldn't believe it.

GINSBERG: Burroughs and I made it a lot over many years, back in 53, so I know his body. And there's the image of the hanged man in Burroughs, the guy that's being hanged and coming involuntarily. At the end of "The Blue Movie" [episode in *Naked Lunch*], there is a sequence of rehearsals over and over again, like cut-ups of the same scene and the same characters over and over: getting hung, and spurting, and the hangman coming up and sucking it, and Mark coming up, and Mary coming up and gobbling up his crotch just as his neck is being snapped, and he's involuntarily coming – just as Burroughs involuntarily comes when being screwed. At the end of that "Blue Movie," they all appear on the screen, bowing, tired, a trickle of saliva, or come, on someone's lower lip, a rope around Johnny's neck, Mary completely worn out and tired. The image is completely washed out through experience.

That's very early Burroughs – 58 or 59 – and leads to more and more cut-ups of his most favorite and tenderly sentimental images. He can finally look at it at the end of the spool; he can look at his most tender, personal, romantic images objectively, and no longer be attached to them. And that's the purpose of the cut-ups: to cut out of habit reactions, to cut through rehearsed habit, to cut through conditioned reflex, to cut out into open space, into endless blue space where there is room for freedom and no obligation to repeat the same image over and over again, to come the same way over and over again.

So Burroughs is one of the very few gay liberation minds who is thinking in ultimate philosophical terms about sexuality, about the nature of "apparent sensory phenomena" (that's his phrase). He's one of the few that has actually questioned sex at the root – not merely rebelled from heterosexual conditioning or heterosexual, social/moral fixed formations – to explore love between men as he has experienced it. He's seen it inside and outside, divine and degraded. But also to go beyond that and look at it through the eyes of a Sufi or a Zen master, or a sufud adept Tibetan monk saying, "Ah."

Burroughs has contributed a great deal of space which a new generation hasn't yet caught up with. His style was picked up by younger people. The whole cut-up-collage thing did influence even underground press writing quite a bit. The further philosophical, practical Yankee examination of sensory phenomena perception that Burroughs had gone into still awaits discovery by the gay lib left. Otherwise, you just get into some kind of a funky scene. There are a lot of young kids who carry sex banners and march around saying sex, sex, sex, great, great, great – doing it humorlessly, reacting to just the initial superficial attraction.

Let's see, what haven't we covered? I asked Swami Shivananda where I could find a guru, and he told me, "Your own heart is your guru." The main slogan, instruction, teaching, compass and fidelity of the whole love situation is the heart which must always be followed because there's no other place to go. And that will dissolve perplexities of ideology, or complexities of the political fix we're into. Following the heart a little more – there's a way of avoiding the pitfalls of hyper-intellectual, ideological dead-ends, which both homosexuals and radicals have gotten into.

Rely on your feelings and trust your feelings. I think a lot of homosexual conflict comes from internalizing society's distrust of your loves, finally doubting your own loves, and therefore not being able to act on them. The other thing is I think it's important to accept rejection because the more you learn to accept rejection, the more you leave yourself vulnerable to be rejected, the more you have a chance of getting laid, of scoring, both for heart and for cock. The more you open yourself up and give yourself, continuously without rancor, and accept rejection from people who are either too timid or are afraid socially, or who just don't want you . . . the more open you'll be to your feelings, the more you'll communicate, the more likely you'll just connect.

One of the greatest difficulties, especially for the younger sexualists of all kinds, is the fear of making a move, because they're afraid of being rejected. So, the only thing is frank revelation of the heart: that applies politically, subjectively, personally . . . It's the lack of trust in the heart that's messed up radical mentality as well as all sexual mentality in America. If we don't interest ourselves in your hearts and accept our hearts, if we don't find our reality in our hearts, then the rest is a perpetual void of intellect, Urizen, Blake's Urizen, your-reason, rationalization, common error, and, ultimately, the heart becomes brightly empty. Thinking of that in terms of making judgments politically: does Tom Forcade have a brightly empty heart, or does he have a heart loaded with silver shit? Is Mark Rudd's heart brightly empty this day as he goes to the anonymous cafeteria for his oatmeal. Is Mother Machree's heart brightly empty as she comes out of the Capri bar at 3 a.m., leaving the most beautiful boy in San Francisco with long curls flowing down his lion-like shoulders with a smile in his eye and pearly teeth showing in the moonlight?

> Beauty is but a flowre,
> Which wrinckles will devoure,
> Brightnesse falls from the ayre,
> Queenes have died yong and faire,
> Dust hath closde *Helens* eye.
> I am sick, I must dye:
> Lord, have mercy on us.

This is "Time of Pestilence" (1593) by Thomas Nashe (1567-1601). It's maybe *the* great poem in the English language, and the greatest line is "Brightnesse falls from the ayre . . . ."

YOUNG: When you traveled to the Soviet Union, what were some of the most significant things you learned there?

GINSBERG: The commonly accepted figure around Moscow, among people who are in the Writers Union, as well as writers who are not members of the Union but are on the outs, but have been in bughouses or in Siberia, is that between 1935 and 1953 under Stalin 20 million Russians were arrested and sent to Siberia and 15 million didn't come back. And then outside the Writers Union, Yessenin-Volpine said the number was 14-15 million, give or take a million. It's the commonly accepted figure around Moscow.

The explanation for the present heaviness in the Russian mentality, compared say with Prague in 1965, or even Cuba, is the "all the bureaucrats who did that are still holding on to their chairs and you have to wait for them to die off." The younger poets think that they'll create a cultural revolution with the young scientists, engineers, physiologists, doctors and athletes who all listen to poetry, and that they'll be more liberal.

One poet in the Writers Union told me that under Stalin almost every family in Moscow had somebody taken away who didn't come back. For instance, Yevtuchenko has people in his family who were taken to Siberia and never returned. One thing I heard was that everybody got it in the neck until there was nobody left, and then the police got it in the neck. Stalin created a whole new sub-bureaucracy of police who arrested the old police, who were compromised by killing everybody. There was a twist in the Party line, so there were perhaps several waves of police who found themselves in the same situation as the people they arrested: themselves under arrest, exiled, with no coming back. The police who are in now, after Krushchev, know that, so they don't want it to go too far any more. The police don't want that kind of absolute, poisonous police state any more with mass secret arrests. So that is a kind of safety brake in Russia – the police realize that they can't go too far or else they'll be swept up in the terror. I've never seen this explained in the West.

YOUNG: Do you think this is an actual reason for the liberalization?

GINSBERG: It's not so much for the liberalization, as a reason why things are not likely to go back to horrific Stalinism. The people that would have to carry out the worst police state orders realize that those orders would finally be carried out against them. Stalin was so strange, so weirdly humored, with such a sinister sense of humor, that no one wants to get into that box again. The police got smart finally, realizing that it was their karma that got trapped.

YOUNG: Did you ever go through a period where you idolized the Soviet Union before you went there?

GINSBERG: No. My mother did. My mother was a Communist in Paterson, New Jersey, and she took me to Communist Party meetings, right off River Street, when I was seven years old, back in 1933. I remember them selling garbanzos. And I heard Israel Amter speak, and Scott Nearing, in those days. In my family, among my aunts in New York and the Bronx, there was an idolization of Stalin, the Party line. My father was against it, as a Socialist. On the other hand, my father went all the way to the other extreme; between 1961 and 1965 he was still backing the war in Vietnam. So between the Scylla of Stalinism and the Charybdis of anti-Stalinism, there was not much of a left in America, really, until the independent hippies came along, with the beatnik really, and introduced a whole new anarchism, which was the old American anarchism like the Wobblies, up to San Francisco and Kenneth Rexroth. That was always a viable tradition of intellectual anarchism, communalism, free love.

YOUNG: Did the 1950s hipsters all think of yourselves as anarchists?

GINSBERG: Oh, yeah. Kenneth Rexroth and Robert Duncan back in 1948-49, in San Francisco (I wasn't there); and in 1943-45 Brother Antoninus and Philip Lamantia, both poets, had an anarchist circle in San Francisco. They were reading Kropotkin, and gay lib was accepted among them. That was the traditional bohemian-Anarchist-West-Coast-Wobbly-Chicago-American Populist [tradition].

YOUNG: What do you mean when you say that gay lib was accepted among them?

GINSBERG: I mean there were all sorts of gay cats around. Robert Duncan was gay and he was a sturdy member of the anarchist circle, I think. The panoply of tolerances and understandings and gnostic (mystic, psychedelic) awarenesses, as well as social hopes and humors, were already fully developed in the 1940s and that continued right on through in San Francisco, and in some circles in New York.

GREY FOX PRESS BOOKS

Robert Creeley *Was That a Real Poem & Other Essays*

Guy Davenport *Herakleitos and Diogenes*

Edward Dorn *Selected Poems*

Allen Ginsberg *The Gates of Wrath: Rhymed Poems* 1948-1952
Gay Sunshine Interview (with Allen Young)
Improvised on the Tongue

Jack Kerouac *Heaven & Other Poems*

Frank O'Hara *Early Writing*
Poems Retrieved
Standing Still and Walking in New York

Charles Olson *The Post Office*

Gary Snyder *He Who Hunted Birds in His Father's Village: The Dimensions of a Haida Myth*

Gary Snyder,
Lew Welch,
Philip Whalen *On Bread & Poetry*

Lew Welch *How I Work as a Poet & Other Essays/Plays/Stories*
I, Leo—An Unfinished Novel
Ring of Bone: Collected Poems 1950-1971
Selected Poems
Trip Trap (with Jack Kerouac & Albert Saijo)

Philip Whalen *Decompressions: Selected Poems*
Scenes of Life at the Capital